This is a Carlton book.

Manufactured and distributed under licence 2013 by Carlton Books Limited

20 Mortimer Street, London W1T 3JW

ISBN 978 1 78312 008 6

10 9 8 7 6 5 4 3 2 1

Printed in China

™ & © 2013 Liverpool Football Club & Athletic Grounds Ltd

A CIP catalogue record for this book is available from the British Library

Written and edited by Emily Stead

Designed by emc Design Limited

PICTURE CREDITS

The publishers would like to thank the following sources for their kind permission to reproduce the pictures in this book.

Imagery © Liverpool Football Club & Athletic Grounds Ltd.
with the following exceptions:

Getty Images: /Clive Brunskill: 88B; /Julian Finney: 84; /Laurence Griffiths: 89B; /Alex Livesey: 90T, 90L; /Bob Thomas: 2-3, 94-95

Images courtesy of Warrior: 5, 15, 20TR, 22TR, 24TR, 26TR, 28TR, 33TR, 35TR, 36TR, 59BL, 59BR, 69T, 85

Every effort has been made to acknowledge correctly and contact the source and/or copyright holder of each picture and Carlton Books Limited apologises for any unintentional errors or omissions that will be corrected in future editions of this book.

★ ★ ★ ★ ★

THE OFFICIAL
Liverpool FC
Ultimate Junior Reds' Book

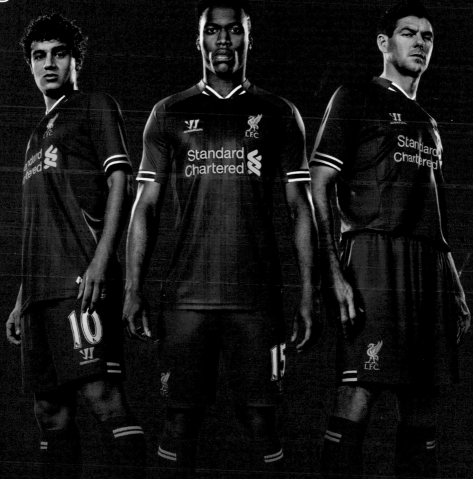

Welcome to the Ultimate Guide to Liverpool Football Club! It's the ultimate book for all junior Reds.

WHAT'S INSIDE?

This is Anfield 8
Mighty Red's Diary 12
Puzzles: Kick-off! 14
Reds Records 18
Steven Gerrard 20
Jose Manuel Reina 22
Lucas Leiva 24
Luis Suarez 26
Daniel Sturridge 28
Stewart Downing 29
Joe Allen 30
Kolo Toure 31
Jordan Henderson 32

Philippe Coutinho	33	Steve McManaman	48
Jose Enrique	34	Billy Liddell	49
Glen Johnson	35	Ian Rush	50
Daniel Agger	36	Robbie Fowler	51
Raheem Sterling	37	Bruce Grobbelaar	52
Brendan Rodgers	38	John Barnes	53
Kenny Dalglish	40	My Dream Team	54
John Aldridge	41	Puzzles: Half-time!	56
Jamie Carragher	42	A–Z of Liverpool FC	60
Roger Hunt	43	Skills School	70
Michael Owen	44	Trophy Cabinet	80
Peter Beardsley	45	Puzzles: Final Whistle!	84
Kevin Keegan	46	Memorable Matches	88
Alan Hansen	47	Puzzle Answers	92

THIS IS ANFIELD

Anfield Stadium, home to Liverpool FC.

Walking into Anfield Stadium is a spine-tingling experience – you can feel the history all around you. An amazing 18 League titles have been won since the club was established back in 1892, and a host of famous players have made their names here, from Ian Rush to Steven Gerrard.

It's not surprising that other teams fear playing at Anfield when over 45,000 loyal fans roar on the Reds at every match.

Anfield's most famous stand is called the Kop, where you'll hear the most famous song in football 'You'll never walk alone' being sung with pride every match. The fans that sit in this mighty terrace are known as 'Kopites' and there are more than 12,000 of them!

REDS TIMELINE

1884 Anfield opens its doors, but as home to Everton FC!

1884 The first match at Anfield sees Everton beat Earlstown 5–0.

DID YOU KNOW?

The club was thinking of building a new stadium in nearby Stanley Park, but have decided to make Anfield even bigger and better instead!

The famous Shankly Gates.

DID YOU KNOW?

Liverpool have not always played in just red. They used to wear white shorts until 1964, when manager Bill Shankly thought an all-red strip would make his team look scarier to the opposition!

The Kop, the largest stand in English football.

1891 Everton move out of the stadium.

1892 Liverpool Football Club is formed as the new team to play at Anfield.

THIS IS ANFIELD

Anfield from the air! A birds-eye view of the famous stadium.

With over 125 years of football matches played at Anfield, you'll find history in every corner of the ground. It's a beautiful ground in which to watch the beautiful game!

Former player/manager and club legend Kenny Dalglish sits in the home dressing room.

The bronze Shankly statue stands by the entrance to the Kop. 'He Made the People Happy' is engraved on its base.

REDS TIMELINE

1952 A record 61,905 pack into Anfield to watch the Reds against Wolves.

1957 Floodlights are installed and used for the first time.

1973 A record highest average attendance of 48,127 is set.

Following the tragedy at Hillsborough Stadium where 96 Liverpool fans lost their lives, a sea of flowers filled the Kop and pitch at Anfield.

THIS IS
LIVERPOOL
FOOTBALL CLUB
ANFIELD

MY FIRST MATCH AT ANFIELD

Complete this fan fill-in if you've visited Anfield!

Date: _____

Score: Liverpool [ ] v _____

Scorers: _____

Attendance: _____

My Match Rating: ★ ★ ★ ★ ★

Luis Suarez touching the famous 'This is Anfield' sign in the players' tunnel. The sign is said to bring the Reds luck and strike fear into their opponents!

Kopites hold up a display reading 'Y N W A (You'll Never Walk Alone), THE KOP' before a Premier League match.

  1982 The Shankly Gates are erected in tribute to legendary manager, Bill Shankly.

 1994 The Kop becomes an all-seater stand.

2013 Anfield has capacity for 45,276 fans to watch a match.

MIGHTY RED'S DIARY

Hi, I'm Mighty Red!

I'm the official mascot to Liverpool Football Club. I'm a super sporty Liver bird who loves nothing more than a good game of footy with my mates.

If you ever visit Anfield on a match day, come and say hello. You can always find me at the Family Park, making friends with fans, warming up the crowd and bringing the players good luck! It's a tough job, but some bird's got to do it!

Why not check out my photo diary to see some of the things I've been up to recently?

You can read more about my adventures online at: **http://www.liverpoolfc.com/kopkids** There are boss videos to watch, great activities and loads more LFC things to do!

See you soon!

Mighty

Mighty Red

MORE ABOUT ME!

Nickname: Mighty

Species: Liver bird

Age: 8

Home town: Liverpool, England

School: St. Anfield Junior School

Family: Liver bird (Dad), Mother Bird (Mum), Ruby Red (little sister), Little Liver (baby brother)

Pets: An iguana called Fred

Hobbies: I enjoy all sports from footie to BMX to riding my scooter. I love to write, too, especially for my website, Kop Kids.

Favourite colour: Red, of course!

DID YOU KNOW THAT I'M ALSO THE MASCOT FOR LIVERPOOL LADIES? I WENT TO THE STOBART STADIUM TO WATCH OUR LADIES PLAY LOCAL RIVALS, EVERTON LADIES!

I LOVE TO PLAY OUTSIDE AND NEVER TURN DOWN A KICK-ABOUT WITH MY MATES!

HERE I AM WITH LFC GOAL MACHINES, ROBBIE FOWLER AND IAN RUSH, ON OUR TOUR OF NORTH AMERICA!

I READ MY NEW MAGAZINE KOP KIDS FROM COVER TO COVER ... TWICE! IT'S PACKED FULL OF COOL STUFF FOR JUNIOR REDS TO READ ABOUT.

Phew! I've been one busy mascot!

PUZZLES: KICK-OFF!

SPOT THE BALL

Take a look at this scene from a Premier League tie against Chelsea.

Where do you think the ball should be?

Tick ONLY the players below if you can see them in the picture.

Jordan Henderson ☐   Dan Agger ☐   Jonjo Shelvey ☐

MIGHTY MIX-UP!

Can you help Mighty find out who these two players are?

Write the names of the players here:

1. _____

2. _____

All the answers
are on pages
92–93

PUZZLES: KICK-OFF!

QUICK QUIZ

Reckon you're the best Reds fan around? Then try your luck at this mega-tough True or False quiz! Tick the boxes to answer true or false to each question.

1. **The Reds play their home games at Stanley Park.**
   true ☐ false ☐

2. **Daniel Sturridge wears the number 23 shirt for Liverpool.**
   true ☐ false ☐

3. **The player shown here is Glen Johnson.**
   true ☐ false ☐

4. **Luis Suarez plays international football for Argentina.**
   true ☐ false ☐

5. **Philippe Coutinho is LFC's most expensive signing.**
   true ☐ false ☐

6. **The Reds have won the League an awesome 18 times!**
   true ☐ false ☐

SOCCER SQUARES

Have a go at completing these tricky Soccer Sudoku puzzles! Remember, each number can appear only once in each column, row and box.

	2		1
4			2
	3		4
1			3

		3	2
1			4
3			
		1		3

		2	4
1			3
4			
		1	3

MIRROR MATCH

Use a mirror to reveal the names of these Liverpool stars, then draw a line to match the names to the players!

REINA   STURRIDGE   COUTINHO

SKRTEL   SUAREZ   GERRARD

REDS RECORDS

Academy graduate Jerome Sinclair is the youngest player ever to represent Liverpool. He made his first-team debut at the age of 16 years 6 days during a League Cup victory over West Brom in 2012.

At the top of the leaderboard of Liverpool appearances made is midfielder Ian Callaghan. He earned a whopping 857 caps playing from 1960–78!

Reds' hero Ian Rush is the club's top scorer in all competitions with an amazing 346 Liverpool goals!

Full back Phil Neal played for Liverpool for nine seasons without missing a single match! He holds the record for the most appearances in a row – 417, from October 1976 to September 1983!

Read on to dazzle your friends and family with your knowledge of the Reds! These record-breaking facts from the club's history books are officially amazing!

The fastest hat-trick for the Reds was scored by Robbie Fowler v Arsenal in 1994. He took just 4 minutes 33 seconds to smash home three goals!

The club's top scorer in Europe is no.8, Steven Gerrard while his long-time team-mate Jamie Carragher holds the record for the most European appearances, racking up 139 over his LFC career.

Liverpool's debut match was played way back in September 1892. It was a friendly v Rotherham Town, which the Reds won 6–1!

RECORD TRANSFERS

IN ⬇
Andy Carroll from Newcastle United
£35m

OUT ⬆
Fernando Torres to Chelsea
£50m

Steven GERRARD

8

> "I was born in Liverpool, I'm a Liverpool supporter."

Steven joined the Liverpool Academy at the age of just nine. Few would have predicted that he would go on to become one of classiest ever players to pull on a Liverpool shirt.

He made his first-team debut on 29 November 1998, and has since made over 400 appearances for the club he supported as a boy.

Gerrard is an explosive, goal-scoring midfielder, who leads by example as the Reds' skipper. The best moment of his Liverpool career was lifting the European Cup in 2005 in Istanbul, though many fans will remember Gerrard scoring a hat-trick against local rivals, Everton, as a highlight. The last time a player did this was back in 1935!

Star man Gerrard also captains his country, England, and has earned over 100 caps playing for the Three Lions.

Player Profile

Squad number:	8
Position:	Midfield
Previous clubs:	None
Nicknames:	Stevie G, Captain Fantastic
Height:	1.83m
Date of birth:	30 May 1980
Place of birth:	Whiston, Merseyside
Nationality:	English

Honours

League Cup: 2000–2001, 2002–2003 2011–2012

FA Cup: 2000–2001, 2005–2006

FA Community Shield: 2001, 2006

UEFA Champions League: 2004–2005

UEFA Cup: 2000–2001

UEFA Super Cup: 2001, 2005

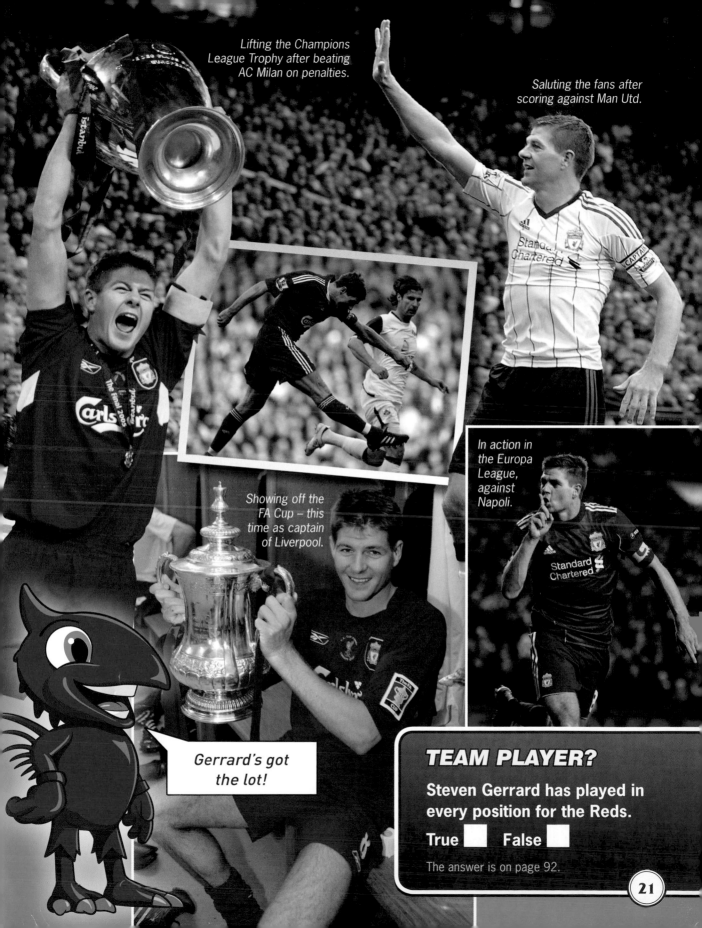

Lifting the Champions League Trophy after beating AC Milan on penalties.

Saluting the fans after scoring against Man Utd.

Showing off the FA Cup – this time as captain of Liverpool.

In action in the Europa League, against Napoli.

Gerrard's got the lot!

TEAM PLAYER?

Steven Gerrard has played in every position for the Reds.

True ☐   False ☐

The answer is on page 92.

21

Jose Manuel REINA

25

Goalkeeper Pepe Reina has been a massive player for Liverpool since he signed for the club in 2005. The Spanish stopper is one of the best 'keepers on the planet and was part of the Spain squad that won the World Cup in 2010 and two European Championships.

The man with the golden gloves is the proud holder of the record as the quickest Liverpool goalie to reach 50 clean sheets. His tally of 50 in 92 matches beats Ray Clemence's record by three matches!

Pepe is known for his lightning-quick reaction saves, excellent distribution from goal kicks, plus he's a brilliant penalty-stopper too. He saved three out of four penalties in the shoot-out that won the Reds the FA Cup in 2006.

If you're wondering where Reina got his skills, his dad was a top 'keeper for Barcelona and Atletico Madrid in the 1960s and 70s. Two number 1s in the same family!

Player Profile

Squad number:	25
Position:	Goalkeeper
Previous clubs:	Barcelona, Villareal
Height:	1.88m
Date of birth:	31 August 1982
Place of birth:	Madrid, Spain
Nationality:	Spanish

Honours

UEFA Intertoto Cup: 2002–03, 2003–04

UEFA Super Cup: 2005

FA Community Shield: 2006

FA Cup: 2006

League Cup: 2012

FIFA World Cup: 2010

UEFA European Championship: 2008, 2012

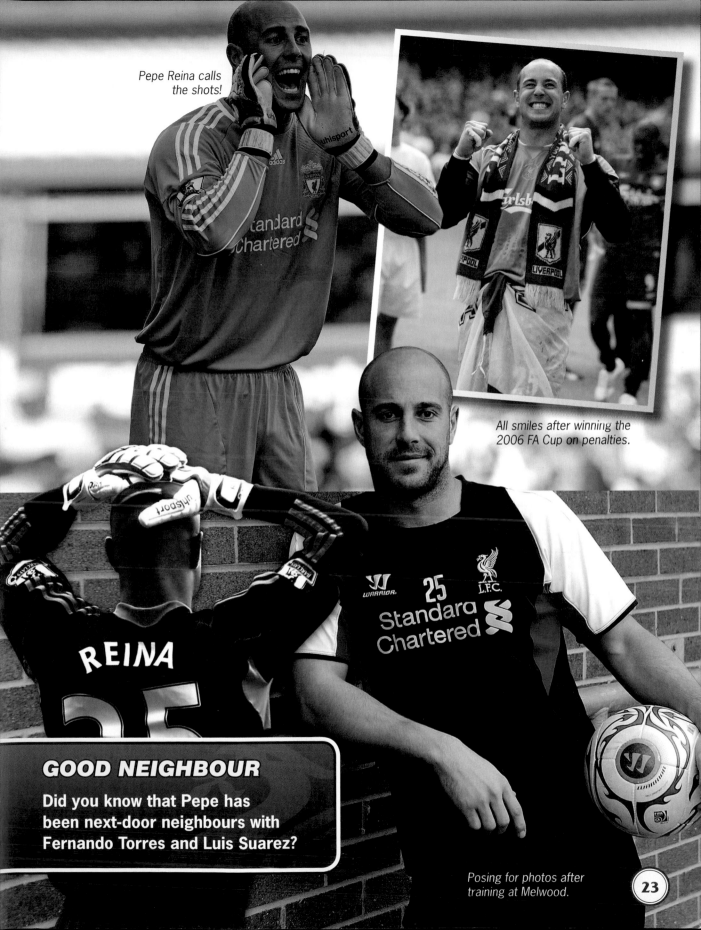

Pepe Reina calls the shots!

All smiles after winning the 2006 FA Cup on penalties.

REINA
25

GOOD NEIGHBOUR

Did you know that Pepe has been next-door neighbours with Fernando Torres and Luis Suarez?

Posing for photos after training at Melwood.

Lucas LEIVA

21

Defensive midfielder Lucas is a key man for the Reds. He is a hard-working player who has lots of stamina and will never stop tackling until the final whistle blows. He joined the club in 2007 for a fee of £5 million, but really made his mark in the centre of Liverpool's midfield when Xabi Alonso left for Real Madrid in 2009.

Lucas has captained Liverpool when Gerrard has been out of the team and admits he loves wearing the captain's armband. In February 2013 Lucas reached the milestone of 200 games for the Reds.

Despite some serious competition from his super-skilful team-mates in the Brazilian national side, he's already won 20 caps for his country. A serious knee injury suffered in 2011 has kept him out of the side, but Lucas hopes his good form will cement his place in the Brazil team again soon.

Player Profile

Squad number:	21
Position:	Midfielder
Previous clubs:	Gremio
Height:	1.79m
Date of birth:	9 January 1987
Place of birth:	Dourados, Brazil
Nationality:	Brazilian

Honours

Serie B:
2005

Campeonato Gaúcho:
2006, 2007

League Cup:
2012

Lucas is always in control

Gooaaalll!

LUCAS 21

Celebrating the 2012 League Cup win!

Lucas loves being a Red!

Lucas at the Liverpool Academy in Kirkby.

We love you, Lucas, we do!

PASSPORT PUZZLER

Although Lucas is Brazilian, he also holds a passport for which European country?

Great Britain ☐   Portugal ☐   Italy ☐

The answer is on page 92.

Luis SUAREZ

7

The middle child of a large family, Luis grew up in Uruguay as part of a ready-made seven-a-side team! Perhaps that's why he wears the number 7 shirt for Liverpool?

The striker has been sensational for the Reds, helping them to win the League Cup in his very first season with the club. He can score from long range, set pieces or in the box with his head and is extremely technically gifted.

Luis left his home country Uruguay for Europe when he was just 19, joining Dutch side Groningen. He played for the club for one season before moving to Ajax, where he played in the Champions League and became the Dutch club's captain. While at Ajax, Luis enjoyed incredible form, scoring 111 goals in 159 appearances.

In 2010, Kenny Dalglish brought Suarez to Anfield. Luis settled at the club quickly and has already scored 50 goals in fewer than 100 appearances for the Reds.

Player Profile

Squad number:	7
Position:	Midfielder
Previous clubs:	Nacional, Groningen, Ajax
Height:	1.81m
Date of birth:	24 January 1987
Place of birth:	Salto, Uruguay
Nationality:	Uruguayan

Honours

KNVB Cup:
2009–10

Eredivisie:
2010–11

League Cup:
2012

Copa America:
2011

Jumping for joy at Anfield!

On the run against Wigan.

SUAREZ
7

SEVENTH HEAVEN

Which of these Liverpool legends did not wear the famous number 7 shirt?

Kevin Keegan [ ]   Jamie Carragher [ ]   Kenny Dalglish [ ]

The answer is on page 92.

Luis in action on his debut v Stoke City.

Daniel STURRIDGE 15

Daniel joined the Reds in January 2013 and was a welcome addition to Liverpool's strikeforce.

A quick, talented forward, Daniel boasts a Champions League title among his medals from his days at Chelsea. He made sure the fans loved him as soon as he arrived at Anfield by scoring in each of his first three matches!

FACT OR FIB?

Daniel is the only Premier League player to have scored on his debut for four different clubs.

True ☐   False ☐

The answer is on page 92.

Player Profile

Squad number: 15
Position: Forward
Previous clubs: Manchester City, Chelsea, Bolton (loan)
Height: 1.83m
Date of birth: 1 September 1989
Place of birth: Birmingham, England
Nationality: English

Honours

Premier League:
2009–10

FA Cup:
2009–10, 2010–11

FA Community Shield:
2009

UEFA Champions League:
2011–12

Stewart DOWNING

13

Wide-man Stewart joined the club from Aston Villa in 2011.

A tasty addition to the Reds' midfield, Downing can play on both the left and right flanks. His creative play and crossing skills make him a tricky winger to play against. He's got bags of pace and is an England international, too!

DID YOU KNOW?

If Stewart wasn't a pro footballer, he'd love to be a DJ!

Player Profile

Squad number:	19
Position:	Midfield
Previous clubs:	Middlesbrough, Sunderland (loan), Aston Villa
Height:	1.80m
Date of birth:	22 July 1984
Place of birth:	Middlesbrough, England
Nationality:	English

Honours

League Cup:
2003–04,
2011–12

Joe ALLEN

Joe swapped Swansea for Liverpool soon after manager Brendan Rodgers became the Anfield gaffer!

A talented young midfielder, Allen is an attack-minded player who is comfortable on the ball. Joe scored his first goal in a Liverpool jersey in January 2013 – a powerful volley against Oldham in the FA Cup.

DID YOU KNOW?

Joe was one of the stars of Team GB's football squad in the London 2012 Olympic Games.

Player Profile

Squad number:	24
Position:	Midfield
Previous clubs:	Swansea City
Height:	1.68m
Date of birth:	14 May 1990
Place of birth:	Camarthen, Wales
Nationality:	Welsh

Honours

League Cup:
2003–04,
2011–12

Kolo TOURE

African defender Toure signed for Liverpool in July 2013 on a free transfer from Manchester City.

He's comfortable on the ball and can play in central defence or at right-back, and arrives at Anfield with loads of experience. Toure has won the League with both of his previous clubs and has a hat-trick of FA Cup medals, too.

BIG BROTHER

Kolo is the older brother of Manchester City midfielder Yaya Toure.

Player Profile

Squad number:	4
Position:	Defender
Previous clubs:	Arsenal, Manchester City
Height:	1.78m
Date of birth:	19 March 1981
Place of birth:	Sokoura Bouake, Ivory Coast
Nationality:	Ivorian

Honours

Premier League:

2003–04,
2011–12

FA Cup:
2002–03,
2004–05,
2010–11

FA Community Shield:
2002, 2004, 2012

Jordan HENDERSON

A playmaking midfielder, one of Jordan's best assets is his ability to create goals for his team-mates.

He signed for Liverpool in June 2011, having played for previous club Sunderland from the age of just seven! He's dangerous from set pieces and has a clever footballing brain.

MIDDLE RIDDLE

Take a guess at Jordan's middle name!

Gordon ☐ Brian ☐ Steven ☐

The answer is on page 92.

Player Profile

Squad number:	14
Position:	Midfield
Previous clubs:	Sunderland, Coventry City (loan)
Height:	1.82m
Date of birth:	17 June 1990
Place of birth:	Sunderland, England
Nationality:	English

Honours

League Cup:
2011–12

Philippe COUTINHO 10

Brilliant Brazilian midfielder Philippe was signed up by Brendan Rodgers in January 2013 and was handed the legendary number 10 shirt.

He's even been compared to Lionel Messi, Barcelona's number 10 – that really is the stuff of legends! Coutinho is the fifth Brazilian to have pulled on a Liverpool shirt. Philippe's creative flair comes in handy for unlocking defences and he likes to chip in with individual goals, too. He scored on his full debut in a 5–0 win over Swansea City.

NAME GAME

Can you guess which nickname below belongs to Philippe?

Bootinho ☐   Showtinho ☐   Pippinho ☐

The answer is on page 92.

Player Profile

Squad number: 10
Position: Midfield
Previous clubs: Vasco da Gama, Inter Milan, Espanyol (loan)
Height: 1.71m
Date of birth: 12 June 1992
Place of birth: Rio de Janeiro, Brazil
Nationality: Brazilian

Honours

Italian Cup:
2010–11

Italian Super Cup:
2010

World Club Cup:
2010

Jose ENRIQUE

3

Jose arrived from Premier League club Newcastle United with bags of experience in the summer of 2011.

His best position is left back, but Jos**e** is an ace left-winger too, thanks to his blistering pace. His nickname is 'El Toro', which means 'the Bull'!

APRIL FOOL?

On 1 April 2012, Enrique had to play in goal after Pepe Reina had been sent off! Is this...

True ☐ False ☐

The answer is on page 92.

Player Profile

Squad number:	3
Position:	Defender
Previous clubs:	Levante, Valencia, Celta Vigo (loan), Villareal, Newcastle Utd
Height:	1.84m
Date of birth:	23 January 1986
Place of birth:	Valencia
Nationality:	Spanish

Honours

League Championship:
2009–10

League Cup:
2011–12

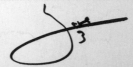

Glen JOHNSON

England right-back Glen arrived at Anfield in 2009 in a big-money move from Portsmouth.

Johnson has won silverware at three of his clubs including back-to-back Championships with Chelsea and the League Cup with Liverpool. He's a pacy defender who loves to be part of the attack, and is comfortable in both the left-back and right-back positions. A class act.

NAME THAT CLUB

From which club did Johnson join Liverpool?

Pompey ☐   The Hammers ☐

The answer is on page 92.

Player Profile

Squad number:	2
Position:	Defender
Previous clubs:	West Ham Utd, Chelsea, Portsmouth
Height:	1.82m
Date of birth:	23 August 1984
Place of birth:	Greenwich, England
Nationality:	English

Honours

Premier League:
2004–05, 2005–06

League Cup:
2004–05, 2011–12

FA Cup:
2008

Daniel AGGER

Centre-back Dan is a Danish international and a strong and powerful stopper in the heart of Liverpool's defence.

An impressive tackler and header of the ball, Dan also shows great technical ability for a central defender. Look out for his rocket of a shot, he can really strike some fierce shots!

STRANGE BUT TRUE!

Daniel has the letters 'Y N W A' tattooed on his knuckles, as a tribute to Liverpool's famous anthem *You'll Never Walk Alone*.

Player Profile

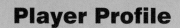

Squad number:	5
Position:	Defender
Previous clubs:	Brondby
Height:	1.91m
Date of birth:	12 December 1984
Place of birth:	Rosenhoj, Denmark
Nationality:	Danish

Honours

Danish Superliga: 2004–05

Danish Cup: 2004–05

FA Cup: 2005–06

FA Community Shield: 2006

League Cup: 2011–12

Standard Chartered

Raheem STERLING

Hotly tipped from the age of 14, Raheem is one to watch!

He joined the Reds in 2010 and made his debut aged 17 years and 107 days – the second-youngest player in Liverpool's history! He's speedy, skilful and has great vision. He earned his first senior England cap at age 18.

WHICH ONE?

Raheem joined the Reds from QPR's Academy. In which city is his former club based?

Manchester ☐ **Bristol** ☐ **London** ☐

The answer is on page 92.

Raheem is one to watch!

Player Profile

Squad number:	31
Position:	Midfield
Previous clubs:	Queens Park Rangers
Height:	1.70m
Date of birth:	8 December 1994
Place of birth:	Kingston, Jamaica
Nationality:	English

Brendan RODGERS

The man in charge of the Reds' team selection, transfers and training is manager, Brendan Rodgers. He's one of the finest young managers around and likes to play a creative, passing style of football. To sum it up, Rodgers loves to play the Beautiful Game!

Brendan began his career as a defender in Northern Ireland, but his playing days were cut short by injury. He moved into management soon after and gained coaching experience working under Jose Mourinho at Chelsea.

He then managed Reading and Watford before a successful spell at Swansea City. Brendan was the first gaffer to get a Welsh team promoted into the Premier League, while at the Liberty Stadium. Some even compared his Swansea side to Barcelona!

After heading to Anfield in the pre-season of 2012–13 he added quality and pace to the Reds' squad, signing Daniel Sturridge and Philippe Coutinho in the January transfer window. His goal is to help Liverpool return to European glory and secure a top-four spot in the Premier League, season after season.

TROPHIES (SO FAR!)

Football League Championship Play-offs 2010–11

Manager Profile

Liverpool career:	1 June 2012–present
Liverpool debut as manager:	2 August 2012, FC Gomel 0–1 Liverpool
Date of birth:	26 January 1973
Previous clubs managed:	Watford, Reading Swansea City
Nationality:	Northern Irish
Nickname:	Buck Rodgers

YOU'LL NEVER WALK ALONE

THIS IS LIVERPOOL FOOTBALL CLUB ANFIELD

Sharing a joke in training with Luis Suarez.

"If you are better than your opponent with the ball, you have a 79% chance of winning the game"

Rodgers has worked with legendary managers Jose Mourinho and World Cup winner Luis Felipe Scolari!

NAME THE NATION

What nationality is Brendan Rodgers?

English ☐   Northern Irish ☐   Scottish ☐

The answer is on page 92.

7

LEGEND

KENNY DALGLISH

Sitting at number 1 in the Liverpool Hall of Fame, Kenny will always be the King of the Kop!

When he arrived at the club from Celtic, he took Keegan's famous number 7 shirt and made it his own. He played for the Reds during a golden age in their history, winning a whole cabinet full of silverware. His vision was his greatest asset and he could create a goal out of nothing. Everything his feet touched turned to gold. In 1985 Kenny became the club's player–manager, then manager, winning three more Championships and two FA Cups. A genius on the pitch and a genius in the dug-out.

Player Profile

Position:	Midfielder
Squad number:	7
Clubs played for:	Glasgow Celtic
Liverpool career:	1977–91
Caps: 515	**Goals:** 172
International team:	Scotland
International caps:	102

HONOURS

Scottish First Division: 1971–72, 1972–73, 1973–74, 1976–77

Scottish Cup: 1971–72, 1973–74, 1974–75, 1976–77

Scottish League Cup: 1974–75

Football League First Division: 1978–79, 1979–80, 1981–82, 1982–83, 1983–84, 1985–86

FA Cup: 1986, 1989

League Cup: 1980–81, 1981–82, 1982–83, 1983–84

Charity Shield: 1977, 1979, 1980, 1982, 1986, 1988, 1989

European Cup: 1977–78, 1980–81, 1983–84

UEFA Super Cup: 1977

MY RATING

COLOUR IN THE STARS TO RATE THIS LEGEND.

JOHN ALDRIDGE

8

LEGEND

John may only have been at Anfield for a short time, but his skill as a striker and brilliant goal-scoring record earns him the title of Liverpool legend.

A Scouser born and bred, John has supported the Reds his whole life, so it was a dream when Kenny Dalglish signed him to replace another goal-ace, Ian Rush. In two years with Liverpool, John won four trophies! Then in 1989 Spanish club Real Sociedad made a massive offer for his services, which was too good for Liverpool to turn down. Aldridge was a hit abroad too, but after two years he returned to Merseyside and signed for Tranmere Rovers.

Player Profile

Position: Forward
Squad number: 8
Clubs played for: South Liverpool, Newport County, Oxford Utd, Real Sociedad, Tranmere Rovers
Liverpool career: 1987–89
Caps: 104   **Goals:** 63
International team: Rep of Ireland
International caps: 69

HONOURS
Welsh Cup: 1979–80
Football League Third Division: 1983–84
Football League Second Division: 1984–85
League Cup: 1985–86
Football League First Division: 1987–88
FA Cup: 1989
Charity Shield: 1988, 1989

MY RATING

COLOUR IN THE STARS TO RATE THIS LEGEND.

41

23

LEGEND

JAMIE CARRAGHER

One of Liverpool FC's ultimate players, Jamie spent his whole career at the club before retiring at the end of the 2012–13 season.

He was an outstanding defender and made over 700 appearances for the Reds, placing him second behind Ian Callaghan on the club's all-time appearance list. Jamie started out as a full back at Liverpool's Academy but later made the central defence position his own. Vice-captain since 2003, 'Carra' was one of the heroes of Istanbul and proudly lifted the European Cup that night with Steven Gerrard.

Player Profile

Position: Defender
Squad number: 23
Clubs played for: Only Liverpool!
Liverpool career: 1996–2013
Caps: 737
Goals: 5
International team: England
International caps: 34

HONOURS

FA Cup:
2001, 2006
League Cup:
2000–01, 2005–06
Community Shield:
2001, 2006
UEFA Champions League:
2004–05
UEFA Cup:
2000–01
UEFA Super Cup:
2001, 2005

MY RATING

COLOUR IN THE STARS TO RATE THIS LEGEND.

8

ROGER **HUNT**

LEGEND

The Reds' leading goalscorer until Ian Rush broke his record, Roger's goals helped Liverpool win promotion back to the top flight before taking two League titles in the sixties and an FA Cup.

The 'Blond Bomber' terrorized defenders and was regularly top scorer thanks to his deadly finishing. Roger was one of the most popular players the club has ever had, and was a key player for the England squad that won the 1966 World Cup too. Wow! He has even been honoured by the Queen for his services to football, so his full title is Roger Hunt, MBE!

Player Profile

Position: Forward
Squad number: 8
Clubs played for: Stockton Heath, Bury, Devizes Town, Bolton, Hellenic FC
Liverpool career: 1958–69
Caps: 492   **Goals:** 286
International team: England
International caps: 34

HONOURS
Football League First Division: 1963–64, 1965–66
Football League Second Division: 1961–62
FA Cup: 1964–65
Charity Shield: 1964, 1965, 1966

MY RATING

COLOUR IN THE STARS TO RATE THIS LEGEND.

43

10

MICHAEL OWEN

LEGEND

Michael Owen is one of Liverpool's greatest-ever young players and was even voted European Player of the Year in 2001, when he won the Ballon d'Or (it means 'Golden Ball' in French!).

Michael loves breaking records! When he scored a wonder goal for England aged just 17, he was the Three Lions' youngest player and goalscorer. He's also the youngest player to have scored 100 Premier League goals! His pace was electric and his finishing was awesome, but sadly injuries cut short a brilliant career and he retired at the end of the 2012–13 season.

Player Profile

Position: Forward

Squad number: 10

Clubs played for: Real Madrid, Newcastle Utd, Manchester Utd, Stoke City

Liverpool career: 1996–2004

Caps: 297   **Goals:** 158

International team: England

International caps: 89

HONOURS

FA Cup: 2000–01

League Cup: 2000–01, 2002–03, 2009–10

Community Shield: 2001, 2010

UEFA Cup: 2000–01

UEFA Super Cup: 2001

Premier League: 2010–11

MY RATING

COLOUR IN THE STARS TO RATE THIS LEGEND.

7

PETER BEARDSLEY

LEGEND

Geordie frontman Peter joined the club in 1987 for what was then a record British transfer fee of £1.9 million.

A brilliant dribbler, he gelled well with new boys Barnes and Aldridge. In Peter's first season at Liverpool he scored 18 goals as Liverpool finished the season as Champions! A second League title followed in 1990. Throughout his career Peter was a joy to watch, whether he was delivering killer passes to his team-mates or slotting home a cool finish under pressure. An Anfield great.

Player Profile

Position: Striker

Squad number: 7

Clubs played for: Carlisle, Vancouver Whitecaps, Manchester United, Newcastle, Everton, Newcastle, Bolton, Man City (loan), Fulham (loan), Hartlepool, Doncaster

Liverpool career: 1987–91

Caps: 175   **Goals:** 59

International team: England

International caps: 59

HONOURS
Football League First Division:
1987–88, 1989–90

FA Cup: 1989

Charity Shield:
1988, 1989, 1990

MY RATING

COLOUR IN THE STARS TO RATE THIS LEGEND.

45

KEVIN KEEGAN

7

LEGEND

Two UEFA Cups, three League titles, a European Cup, an FA Cup and a century of Liverpool goals: it's not surprising that magical midfielder Kevin makes it into our Legends team.

A footballing superstar, Kevin was so famous, you could call him the David Beckham of the seventies! The Kop loved Keegan for his energy, skills and, of course, goals! In 1977 he moved to German giants Hamburg, where he was crowned European Footballer of the Year twice and won the German League title. When his playing days were over, Kevin became a coach, most famously managing Newcastle United and England.

Player Profile

Position: Midfielder/Forward
Squad number: 7
Clubs played for: Scunthorpe Utd, Hamburg SV, Southampton, Newcastle Utd
Liverpool career: 1971–77
Caps: 323   **Goals:** 100
International team: England
International caps: 63

HONOURS

Football League First Division: 1972–73, 1975–76, 1976–77
FA Cup: 1974
Charity Shield: 1974, 1976
European Cup: 1977
UEFA Cup: 1973, 1976
German Bundesliga: 1978–79

MY RATING

COLOUR IN THE STARS TO RATE THIS LEGEND.

ALAN HANSEN

6

LEGEND

Before his days as a football pundit, Alan spent thirteen thrilling seasons as a classy centre-half for Liverpool.

Not your average central defender, he was graceful, skilful and could read the game superbly. He was cool under pressure and liked to pass and move out of defence rather than clear the ball straight away. Alan boasts one of the best medal collections in the game including eight awesome League titles and three European Cups. 1985–86 was probably his best season, as Hansen captained the Reds to their first-ever Double. A dream defender.

Player Profile

Position: Defender
Squad number: 6
Clubs played for: Partick Thistle
Liverpool career: 1977–91
Caps: 620   **Goals:** 14
International team: Scotland
International caps: 26

HONOURS

Scottish First Division: 1975–76
Football League First Division: 1978–79, 1979–80, 1981–82, 1982–83, 1983–84, 1985–86, 1987–88, 1989–90
FA Cup: 1986, 1989
League Cup: 1980–81, 1981–82, 1982–83, 1983–84
Charity Shield: 1978, 1980, 1981, 1983, 1987, 1990
European Cup: 1977–78, 1980–81, 1983–84
UEFA Super Cup: 1985–86

MY RATING

COLOUR IN THE STARS TO RATE THIS LEGEND.

7

STEVE McMANAMAN

A wizard of a right winger, Steve could cast spells on defenders! He joined the club aged 14 and soon became a teenage sensation.

He could switch between the left and right wings, play in central midfield or just behind the forwards – he caused trouble for opponents whatever his position! The highlight of his Liverpool career was his two goals in Liverpool's League Cup win over Bolton in 1995 – fans named the match 'the McManaman Final'. Macca has won the most trophies of any British player to play overseas, including the Champions League twice with Real Madrid.

Player Profile

Position: Midfielder

Squad number: 7

Clubs played for: Real Madrid, Manchester City

Liverpool career: 1990–99

Caps: 364 **Goals:** 66

International team: England

International caps: 37

HONOURS

FA Cup: 1992

League Cup: 1995

La Liga: 2000–01, 2002–03

Supercopa de España: 2001, 2003

UEFA Champions League: 2000, 2002

UEFA Super Cup: 2002

Intercontinental Cup: 2002

MY RATING

COLOUR IN THE STARS TO RATE THIS LEGEND.

BILLY LIDDELL

9

LEGEND

Not many footballers have played for the same club for four different decades – but Billy Liddell was a Red from the 1930s to the 1960s.

That's amazing! Billy was a thrilling, two-footed, skilful winger. His trademark was his thunderbolt strike that almost burst the opposition's net! Like many players of his generation Billy's football career was interrupted by World War II, but he returned to the game and was such a gentleman that he was never booked during his whole career. He was a well-respected captain and some fans even nicknamed the club 'Liddellpool' in his honour!

Player Profile

Position: Midfielder/Forward

Squad number: 9

Clubs played for: Kingseat Juveniles, Lochgelly Violet; Chelsea, Linfield, Cambridge Town, Toronto Scottish and Dunfermline (wartime guest)

Liverpool career: 1939–61

Caps: 534   **Goals:** 228

International team: Scotland

International caps: 6

HONOURS

English First Division:
1946–47

MY RATING

COLOUR IN THE STARS TO RATE THIS LEGEND.

9

IAN RUSH

LEGEND

Welshman Ian was quite simply a goal machine!

He's the Reds' all-time leading scorer with 346 goals – a club record that will take some beating. Although he didn't look the part when he broke into the team as a tall, thin young striker, once he started scoring he just couldn't stop! Rush had electric pace and was tricky to mark, plus his striking partnership with Kenny Dalglish was one of the best ever. He won an amazing 18 major trophies while at Anfield, before leaving in a big-money move to Italian giants, Juventus. But he couldn't stay away for long – he returned to Anfield and played another 245 times for the Reds!

Player Profile

Position: Forward

Squad number: 9

Clubs played for: Chester, Juventus, Leeds, Newcastle, Sheffield United (loan), Wrexham, Sydney Olympic

Liverpool career: 1980–96

Caps: 660 **Goals:** 346

International team: Wales

International caps: 73

HONOURS
Football League First Division: 1981–82, 1982–83, 1983–84, 1985–86, 1989–90

FA Cup: 1986, 1989, 1992

League Cup: 1980–81, 1981–82, 1982–83, 1983–84, 1994–95

FA Charity Shield: 1982, 1986, 1990

European Cup: 1980–81, 1983–84

MY RATING

COLOUR IN THE STARS TO RATE THIS LEGEND.

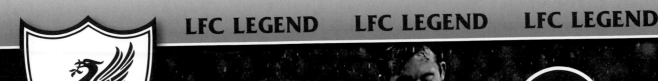

LEGEND

ROBBIE FOWLER

9

A natural finisher, Robbie scored close to 200 goals for the club during his Liverpool career.

He may not have been the tallest of strikers, but he more than made up for it by always being in the right place at the right time to score a goal – from tap-ins to torpedo-like strikes from outside the box! He regularly scored over 30 goals a season for the Reds, earning him the nickname of 'God'! Kop fans were delighted when Robbie returned to Anfield on a free transfer under Rafa Benitez.

Player Profile

Position: Forward

Squad number: 9

Clubs played for: Leeds United, Manchester City, Cardiff City, Blackburn Rovers, North Queensland Fury

Liverpool career: 1992–2007

Caps: 369   **Goals:** 183

International team: England

International caps: 26

HONOURS
FA Cup: 2001

League Cup: 1994–95, 2000–01

Charity Shield: 2000–01

UEFA Cup: 2000–01

UEFA Super Cup: 2000–01

MY RATING

COLOUR IN THE STARS TO RATE THIS LEGEND.

1

BRUCE GROBBELAAR

Probably the most wobbly-legged keeper in the history of football, Bruce was a genius in goal and a real showman too!

After making his Reds debut he went almost FIVE years without missing a match. He turned out for Liverpool for 14 years in a team that won trophy after trophy. Bruce's most famous performance was in the 1984 European Cup Final when his goal-line antics caused a Roma player to fluff his penalty and lose the penalty shoot-out. Liverpool won the European Cup for the fourth time!

Player Profile

Position: Goalkeeper

Squad number: 1

Clubs played for: Vancouver Whitecaps, Crewe (loan), Stoke (loan), Southampton, Plymouth, Oxford, Sheff Wed, Oldham, Chesham, Bury, Lincoln, Northwich Victoria

Liverpool career: 1981–94

Caps: 628 **Goals:** 0

International team: Zimbabwe

International caps: 33

HONOURS

Football League First Division:
1981–82, 1982–83, 1983–84, 1985–86, 1987–88, 1989–90

FA Cup: 1986, 1989, 1992

League Cup: 1982, 1983, 1984

FA Charity Shield:
1986, 1988, 1989, 1990

European Cup:
1984

European Super Cup:
1986

MY RATING

COLOUR IN THE STARS TO RATE THIS LEGEND.

10

JOHN BARNES

LEGEND

The king of dribbling, John Barnes remains one of the most important players in the Reds' history.

John Barnes was one of the most naturally gifted wingers in the club's history. 'Digger' began his career in left midfield and had bags of strength and skill, as well as one of the sweetest left feet around. His link-up play with fellow attackers Aldridge and Beardsley saw John score over 100 goals for Liverpool. Adored by the crowd, he won two League Championships while with the Reds.

Player Profile

Position: Midfielder
Squad number: 10
Clubs played for: Watford, Newcastle Utd, Charlton Athletic, Celtic
Liverpool career: 1987–97
Caps: 407 **Goals:** 108
International team: England
International caps: 79

HONOURS
Football League First Division:
1987–88, 1989–90

FA Cup: 1989, 1992

League Cup: 1994–95

FA Charity Shield:
1989, 1990, 1991

MY RATING

COLOUR IN THE STARS TO
RATE THIS LEGEND.

MY ANFIELD DREAM TEAM

LB

CB

GK

CB

RB

Now you know all about today's top Reds and the club's all-star greats it's your turn to step into the manager's dug-out and create your own squad of Anfield legends!

Choose any player you like when building your very own dream team – top players present or past, your friends, family or even yourself! Then think of a special skill for each player.

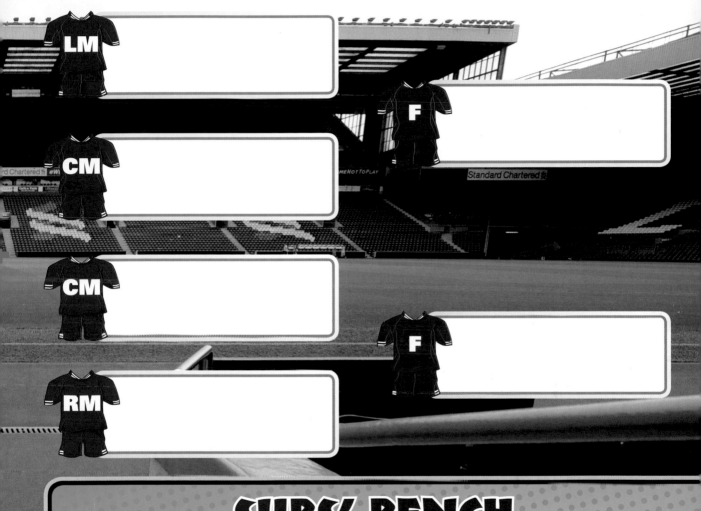

LM

F

CM

CM

F

RM

SUBS' BENCH

MANAGER

SUBS

PUZZLES: HALF-TIME!

SQUAD SUMS

Know your squad numbers? Take the numbers test here!

Write the player's name and his squad number on the blank shirt!

A JOHNSON **2** + AGGER **5** + GERRARD **8** =

B COUTINHO **10** − SUAREZ **7** − JONES **1** =

C ASSAIDI **11** X ENRIQUE **3** =

D LUCAS **21** − HENDERSON **14** =

SPOT THE DIFFERENCE

There are six differences between these pictures from Liverpool's recent clash with Queens Park Rangers. Can you spot them all?

Picture 1

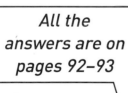

All the answers are on pages 92–93

Picture 2

PUZZLES: HALF-TIME!

ON THE VOLLEY!

Stevie G smashes home a vicious volley! These pictures of Stevie may look alike, but one is different from the rest. Can you spot the odd one out?

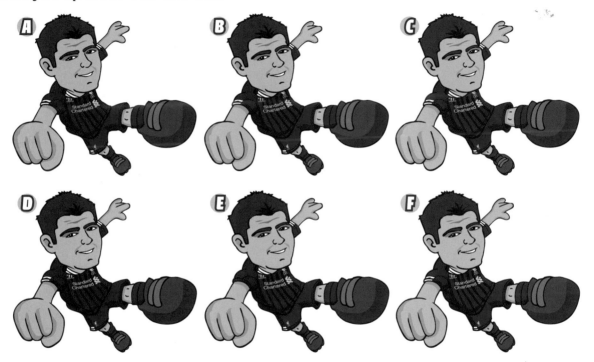

PLAYER PUZZLER

Read the clues and work out which Red is talking here. As soon as you think you know, write the name in the space.

A I joined the Reds back in 2007.

B I play in midfield.

C I'm one of Liverpool's boys from Brazil!

D My squad number is higher than 20.

FLAG TAG!

Draw lines to match each player to his country's flag.

AN A-Z OF LIVERPOOL FC

A is for... Anfield

Awesome Anfield is one of the oldest stadiums in the Premier League. Full of history, the grand ground has hosted thousands of memorable matches since 1884. Home to the famous Kopites, their legendary support makes Anfield Stadium one of the toughest places for away teams to come and play.

You've read about brilliant Barnes, our second entry in this A–Z of the club. The Jamaican-born dribbler was one of the best players in the world during the 1980s and 90s, and will forever be loved by Liverpool fans. The tastiest of number 10s would push for a place in any great Reds' side of the past.

B is for... Barnes

60

C

is for...
Callaghan

The man who has made the most appearances for Liverpool FC. With a staggering 857 caps over 18 years with the club, Ian Callaghan's remarkable record will be almost impossible to beat. He played right midfield for the club between 1960 and 1978 and was a star in Bill Shankly's glorious team of the sixties.

D

is for...
Dalglish

Kenneth Mathieson Dalglish or King Kenny as he's known by all at Anfield will forever be found in Liverpool's hall of fame. The free-scoring Scot was a pure genius on the ball and oozed quality with every kick. What he went on to achieve as manager made sure he'll always be an Anfield legend. Simply the best!

E

is for...
European Cup

A competition that Liverpool have won a fantastic five times in their history – the most wins of any British club. Their first trophy was won in 1977 when Liverpool beat German team, Borussia Mönchengladbach 3–1. They retained the Cup the following season, beating Bruges. They were champions again in 1981 and 1984, beating Real Madrid and Roma, before the magical win over AC Milan in 2005!

61

F
is for...
First Division

Before the Premier League began, the top flight in English football was called the First Division. All 18 of Liverpool's titles were as winners of the First Division. The club kicked off its winning ways in 1900–01 and dominated the Division in the sixties, seventies and eighties. The most recent title came in 1989–90, when the Reds won the League by 9 points and John Barnes finished as top scorer!

G
is for...
Gerrard

It had to be Stevie, Liverpool's inspirational skipper, for the letter G! The mega midfielder has collected almost every medal during his 15 years with Liverpool. The only one he's missing is the Premier League title, which he would love to add. His superb performance in the Champions League Final in 2005 will forever be talked about by Liverpool fans!

H
is for...
Hunt

Sixties superhero Roger Hunt was an outstanding Liverpool player and England World Cup winner. He wasn't spotted until he was 21, while playing for an amateur side. Once he'd made his debut for the Reds, though, he didn't stop scoring for a decade! To this day Roger has still scored the most League goals of any Liverpool player.

I

is for...
Istanbul

On the 25 May 2005, a very special match took place at the Olympic Stadium in Istanbul, Turkey. The Champions League Final was a tense affair between Liverpool and favourites, AC Milan. When Milan went 3–0 up in the first half, everyone thought that Liverpool had lost until the Reds fought back! After 90 minutes, the score was 3–3. A penalty shoot-out saw Liverpool win 3–2 to lift the trophy for a fantastic fifth time!

J

Mop-topped midfielder Craig Johnston was one of the first Australian players to make a major impact in English football. Plucked from Middlesbrough, Johnston had already made 60 League appearances when he signed for the Reds, aged 20. His tireless running made him a big hit with the fans. After he retired he worked as a football boot designer!

is for...
Johnston

K

is for...
Kop

The Spion Kop at Anfield is one of the most famous stands in world football. Over the years it has been redeveloped, knocked down and changed from standing room only to an all-seater stand, but its atmosphere has stayed the same – incredible! Fans who sit in the Kop are known as Kopites. They are the supporters who have helped make Anfield a fortress, singing their famous songs from kick-off until the final whistle!

L

is for...
Liver Bird

The famous bird on the Reds' crest is the Liver bird, which is also the symbol of the city of Liverpool. It first took its perch on the players' shirts for the 1950 FA Cup Final and has been the club's mascot ever since. You've met mascot Mighty Red. He's the loudest Liver bird around!

M is for... Merseyside Derby

Some cracking matches have been played between the two top sides in the city over the years! Neighbours Liverpool and Everton are fierce rivals, with their grounds less than 1km apart. No matter what the form of either team going into a Merseyside derby, you're guaranteed a competitive match.

N is for... Neal

Right-back Phil Neal is the most decorated player in the history of Liverpool FC! In fact, he's got more medals than any other Englishman, all 23 of them earned from his playing days for the Reds during the seventies and eighties. He notched up an impressive 650 appearances for the club and scored 60 goals – not bad for a full-back! A legendary number 2.

O is for... Owen

The boy wonder Michael Owen was a marvellous player for the Reds. He played a big part in the cup Treble of 2001. It was Owen's two late goals in the FA Cup Final that won the match that year. Speed and goal-poaching were his greatest skills, and earned him contracts at some of the biggest clubs in Europe – from Liverpool to Real Madrid.

P is for... Paisley

Bob Paisley lived and breathed Liverpool! He joined the Reds as a defender in 1939, then had a spell as the club's physio before later becoming the manager! He loved Liverpool so much that he stayed at the club for almost fifty years. Bob was the boss when the Reds enjoyed a sensational period in their history in the seventies, winning 14 major trophies including three European Cups and six League titles.

Q is for... Quality

A club that has won 18 titles and five European Cups in its history could not have done this without playing quality football. From the training ground at Melwood to match days at Anfield, Liverpool try to play a brand of exciting, attacking football. The club has always looked to sign quality players too, from Kenny Dalglish to Luis Suarez.

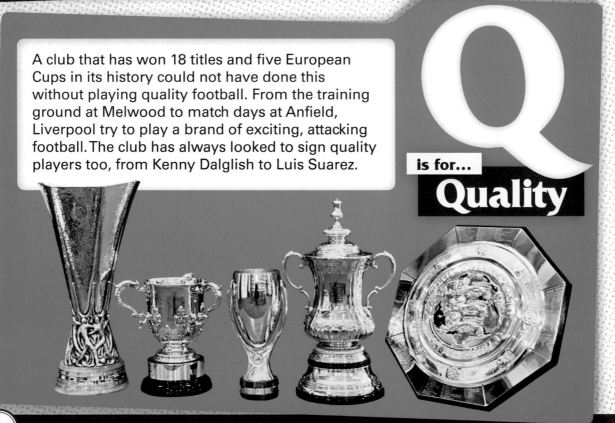

R is for... Rush

The most famous man to wear the number 9 shirt at Liverpool, Ian Rush was a superb striker. He was signed from Chester City for £300,000 – a world record for a teenager back then! Rush enjoyed two spells at the club and scored a staggering 346 goals. He has also scored the most goals in Merseyside derbies – he found the back of the net 25 times against Everton!

S is for... Shankly

Possibly the best football manager ever, Bill Shankly took charge of the Reds when they were in the Second Division and made them one of the best teams in the club's history. Promotion in his first season gave the players their first taste of success, as ten more trophies followed during his reign, including Liverpool's first silverware in Europe. Shanks is so famous he even got his own stamp in 2013 – first-class, of course!

T is for... Treble

The first season of the new millennium was a memorable one for LFC. Managed by Frenchman Gerard Houllier, the Reds landed a unique cup Treble, winning the FA Cup, League Cup and UEFA Cup. Liverpool were once again feared in Europe as well as at home. The club's first Treble came in 1984 when the club won the League, League Cup and European Cup!

U

is for...
UEFA Cup

Three-time winners of the UEFA Cup, Liverpool twice won the competition in the 1970s before making it third time lucky in 2001 when the Reds beat Spanish side Alaves. The match was a thriller as the score finished 5–4 after extra-time. Man of the match was Scot Gary McAllister, who scored Liverpool's third.

V

is for...
Victory

| LIVERPOOL | 11 |
| STRØMSGODSET | 0 |

From narrow wins to bumper scores, victory is what the Reds strive for in every match in which they are involved. Check out the club's record victory, from the European Cup Winners' Cup competition back in 1974!

W

is for...
Wembley

Wembley Stadium is almost like a second home for Liverpool FC! The club has played some thrilling finals there and lifted League Cups, FA Cups and even the European Cup in 1978. Perhaps the win that meant the most to the fans and players was when the Reds won the FA Cup on 20 May 1989, just five weeks after the tragedy at Hillsborough.

If you were in the manager's hot seat at Anfield, who would make it into your first XI of Liverpool's greatest-ever players? Try creating your own fantasy Dream Team on pages 54–55. Choose your favourite heroes from the current LFC squad or even club

is for...
X
XI

Hearing the famous anthem of Liverpool FC sung by 45,000 fans on a match day is guaranteed to send shivers down your spine! It's one of the best-known songs in football and was first adopted by Reds fans way back in the 1960s! The words also appear on Anfield's famous Shankly Gates.

is for...
Y
You'll Never Walk Alone

is for...
Z
Zimbabwe

The nationality of Liverpool's most colourful keeper, Bruce Grobbelaar. Born in South Africa, Bruce moved to neighbouring country Zimbabwe (known then as Rhodesia) as a baby. Bruce made over 500 appearances for Liverpool, winning a European Cup, six League titles, three FA Cups and three League Cups.

L.F.C. SKILLS SCHOOL

THE LIVERPOOL WAY

Welcome to Liverpool FC's Skills School, where you can improve your skills with advice from the experts. First, let's learn how to play the Liverpool Way...

The coaches at Liverpool FC pride themselves on producing world-class players and delivering exciting football to fans.

It takes time to develop younger players to ensure that they reach their full potential. The Skills School guides them through expert training programmes and nurtures their development. This way, Liverpool FC has produced some of the best players in the world over the years – from Steven Gerrard and Jamie Carragher to new talent like Raheem Sterling and Martin Kelly.

To be a part of Liverpool Football Club is a great honour, and following the Liverpool Way means hard work, fair play and respectful behaviour on and off the pitch. Everyone should be aware of the traditions and standards that the club represents.

www.liverpoolfc.com/soccerschools

WARMING UP

Warming up is essential before training and matches to make sure your body and mind are in the game. Your heart rate should increase and your muscles and joints should be working freely.

Start with some light running and slowly build up your speed to include some short sprints. Next, work on warming up your muscles. Hold each stretch for ten seconds.

Remember to warm down after sessions, too!

WARM UP YOUR...

QUADS for striking the ball

HAMSTRINGS for when you're accelerating away on or off the ball

CALVES for your all-round play

GROINS for when you suddenly change direction

HIPS for when you twist and turn on the ball

TAKE ON FLUIDS

Remember to keep your drinks bottle topped up to keep you hydrated and replace the fluids you'll lose through sweating.

LISTEN IN

Respect your coaches and listen to their advice – they are in charge!

PRACTISE, PRACTISE, PRACTISE

Even the best players in the world need to train hard to be at the top of their game.

L.F.C. SKILLS SCHOOL

SOLID DEFENSIVE HEADERS

Check out this smart advice on how to head the ball when playing in defence...

For a defender, the aim is to head the ball as high and as far away from the goal as possible. Here are three tips to help you do that...

1

Watch the flight of the ball and get into position.

2

Jump into the flight of the ball and keep your eyes open.

3

Head the ball with the centre of your forehead, aiming for the bottom half of the ball, then try to send it far away from goal.

AWESOME ATTACKING HEADERS

Luis Suarez is a superb header of the ball. Here's how he uses his head to score a goal…

The aim here is to head the ball downwards towards the goal and give yourself the best possible chance of scoring. Here are three top moves…

1 Get into position, be positive and attack the ball at the right moment.

2 Head the ball with your forehead and try to send it downwards.

3 Aim for the corners of the goal – they're the hardest areas for the goalkeeper to reach for a save.

L.F.C. SKILLS SCHOOL

DREAM TEAM DRIBBLING

Wing-man Stewart Downing is an expert dribbler. You can be an ace on the ball too!

Dribbling is all about keeping possession of the ball while moving it up the pitch.

1 Set off on a run keeping the ball close to your feet. Take lots of little touches with your laces to keep the ball under control.

2 Keep your head up so you can see oncoming defenders, and decide what to do with the ball.

3 When you feel confident at basic dribbling, practise changing direction, injecting speed and using different parts of the foot to move the ball.

L.F.C. SKILLS SCHOOL

PERFECT PENALTIES

Skipper Stevie G is a star at spot-kicks. Here's how to keep your cool like he does.

From the second the penalty is awarded by the ref, try to block out everything around you. Relax and take a few deep breaths.

1 Decide where you're going to place the ball in the goal – and stick to your decision. Aiming for the corners makes it hardest for the keeper to save your penalty shot.

2 Don't make eye contact with the keeper or look at where you want the ball to go – concentrate on the ball when you're taking the kick.

3 Strike the ball firmly and with confidence. And remember, the more you practise, the more comfortable you'll be at taking spot-kicks.

L.F.C. SKILLS SCHOOL

SHARP SHOOTING

Striker Daniel Sturridge is always hungry for goals! Here are tips on how you too can become a sharp shooter...

All strikers love to score goals. If you don't take a shot, you'll never score. When you find yourself in a goal-scoring position, remember these tips...

1

Take a look to make sure you're aware of your position relative to the goal.

2

Choose the right technique for the shot: side-foot the ball for accuracy or use the instep (laces) and follow through for a powerful strike.

3

Concentrate on hitting the target, remembering to keep your head down and your eyes on the ball. Stay relaxed and make as clean contact with the ball as you can.

L.F.C. SKILLS SCHOOL

WICKED ONE-ON-ONES

Ever wondered how to beat the opposition in a tricky one-on-one? Here's how to do it with confidence like Coutinho's...

Here are some tips for a one-on-one when you only have a single defender or the goalkeeper to beat. Attacking players are most likely to find themselves in this situation.

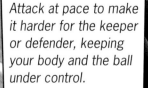

2

Attack at pace to make it harder for the keeper or defender, keeping your body and the ball under control.

1

This skill is all about instinct and belief in yourself. Try to stay cool and confident – and believe you will score.

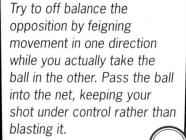

3

Try to off balance the opposition by feigning movement in one direction while you actually take the ball in the other. Pass the ball into the net, keeping your shot under control rather than blasting it.

L.F.C. SKILLS SCHOOL

COOL KEEPY-UPS

Jordan Henderson is the king of keepy-ups! Here's how to juggle the ball with style...

Being able to control the ball well affects every move you make on the pitch.

1

To practise juggling the ball start by using one or both feet, and allow yourself one touch of the ball in between touches.

2

As your skills develop, try to use fewer bounces until you can juggle the ball without any bounces at all.

3

Add touches with your chest, your head and thighs as your confidence grows.

78

L.F.C. SKILLS SCHOOL

MY CHECKLIST

The only way to improve your skills is to practise, practise, practise! Tick off the skills below once you have read the tips from the LFC stars and practised the skills for yourself. Then add a toughness rating for each skill.

WARMING UP WITH STEVEN GERRARD

Toughness:

SOLID DEFENSIVE HEADERS WITH DANIEL AGGER

Toughness:

AWESOME ATTACKING HEADERS WITH LUIS SUAREZ

Toughness:

DREAM TEAM DRIBBLING WITH STEWART DOWNING

Toughness:

PERFECT PENALTIES WITH STEVEN GERRARD

Toughness:

SHARP SHOOTING WITH DANIEL STURRIDGE

Toughness:

WICKED ONE-ON-ONES WITH PHILIPPE COUTINHO

Toughness:

COOL KEEPY-UPS WITH JORDAN HENDERSON

Toughness:

TROPHY CABINET

From the club's first major trophy in 1901 – the first of an amazing 18 League titles – to the amazing night of European glory in Istanbul, Liverpool FC are one of the most successful clubs in world football. Here are some highlights from the Reds' bulging trophy cabinet!

LIVERPOOL FC'S SILVERWARE... IN NUMBERS

18 League Titles

5 European Cups

7 FA Cups

8 League Cups

3 UEFA Cups

3 UEFA Super Cups

15 Community Shields

4 Second Division Titles

Euro Glory

Liverpool have won the European Cup five times – that's more than any other English club! When they beat AC Milan in the Champions League Final in 2005 it was the fifth time the Reds had won the Cup. Liverpool were awarded their own trophy to keep for ever!

The fifth Cup takes a holiday!

Jamie's Joy

Carra was captain when Liverpool lifted the UEFA Super Cup in 2005 in Monaco! The Reds beat CSKA Moscow 3 – 1 after extra time!

DID YOU KNOW?

Former no.9 Ian Rush has scored the most FA Cup and League Cup goals for the club – 87 in total!

High Five!

The five, yes FIVE, trophies that Liverpool won in the year 2001! From left to right: the UEFA Cup, the League Cup, the UEFA Super Cup, the FA Cup and the Community Shield!

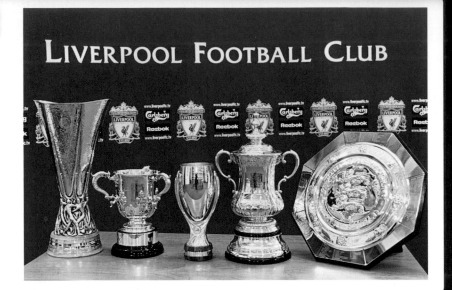

Cup Kings

From the first FA Cup win at Wembley Stadium in 1965… … to the latest victory at the Millennium Stadium in 2006, Liverpool have won a sensational seven FA Cups!

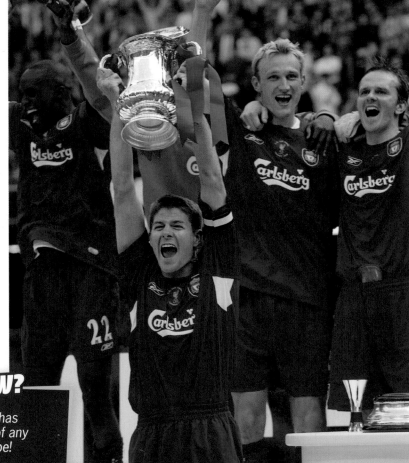

DID YOU KNOW?

Captain Steven Gerrard has scored the most goals of any Liverpool player in Europe!

Champions!

John Barnes celebrates winning the League. Liverpool were most recently Champions in 1989–90. Before the days of the Premier League, this trophy, known as the 'Old Lady', was awarded to the winners of the League!

DID YOU KNOW?

You can see the famous trophies for yourself at the Liverpool FC Museum at Anfield Stadium!

On Parade

King Kenny was a key player in the Double cup-winning season 1985–86, when Liverpool landed the League and FA Cups!

King Kenny on the Double winners' cup parade when Liverpool won the League and FA Cup Double in 1986!

Treble Tour

The Reds won a historic treble in 1984, recording victories in the League, League Cup and European Cup! What a season!

PUZZLES: FINAL WHISTLE!

MISSING MIGHTY!

Mighty has taken his seat in the Kop before kick-off! Can you spot him among the Liverpool crowd?

MIGHTY'S MEMORY TEST

Just how good is your memory? Put it to the test with Mighty's brain-busting puzzle. Study everything on this page for two minutes then turn over the page. See how many questions you can answer.

All the answers are on pages 92-93

PUZZLES: FINAL WHISTLE!

MEMORY TEST

Grab a pen and piece of paper and try to answer the ten questions below.
How much do you remember?

1 **How many footballs were on the page?**

_____

2 **Which number was backwards?**

_____

3 **What colour shirt was Reina wearing?**

_____

4 **How many trophies did you count?**

_____

5 **What colour were Jonjo Shelvey's shorts?**

_____

6 **How many players were wearing the Liverpool home kit?**

_____

7 **Who was wearing a training kit?**

_____

8 **How many corner flags were there?**

_____

TIME'S UP

Stop the clock! Can you write digital versions of these match-day times?

A

B

C

_____ : _____   _____ : _____   _____ : _____

PICTURE PATTERNS

Puzzle over these picture patterns! Can you work out which picture should come next in each row?

1

2

3

4

MEMORABLE MATCHES

From European glory to magical Merseyside derbies, we look back at some of the very best Liverpool performances of the last decade. How many of these matches do you remember? Why not ask the older Reds fans in your family if they can remember any of these famous fixtures, too?

2002–2003 Season

Date: 2 March, 2003

Score: Liverpool 2–0 Manchester United

Competition: League Cup

A worthy win over rivals Manchester United secured a seventh League Cup for Liverpool. Goals from superstars Steven Gerrard and Michael Owen sealed the victory.

2003–2004 Season

Date: 30 August, 2003

Score: Everton 0–3 Liverpool

Competition: Premier League

A brilliant victory over arch-rivals Everton at Goodison Park was the season's highpoint in 2003–04. Two goals from goal-king Michael Owen put Liverpool ahead before Harry Kewell wrapped up the win with his first goal for the Reds.

The players line up to decide the penalty shoot-out.

2004–2005 Season

Date: 25 May, 2005

Score: AC Milan 3–3 Liverpool (2–3 penalties)

Competition: Champions League

It had to be Istanbul! The miracle comeback from 3–0 down was masterminded by Rafa Benitez in his debut season at the club. It was the fifth time Liverpool had won the European Cup in their history and one of the most exciting Champions League matches in the competition's history!

2005–2006 Season

Date: 13 May, 2006

Score: Liverpool 3–3 West Ham United (3–1 penalties)

Competition: FA Cup

Liverpool beat West Ham after a gripping penalty shoot-out In the FA Cup Final at the Millennium Stadium in Cardiff. The game became known as the Gerrard final as he saved Liverpool from defeat right at the end.

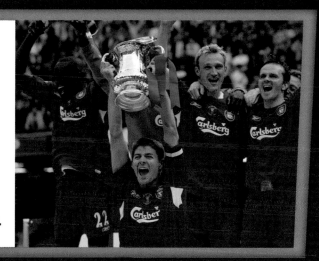

2006–2007 Season

Date: 23 May, 2007

Score: AC Milan 2–1 Liverpool

Competition: Champions League

Following a brilliant run in the Champions League, Liverpool were pipped to the cup by Milan in the Final. The Italian side were out for revenge after losing to Liverpool in the Final two seasons earlier. Kuyt scored a late goal but the Reds just missed out.

2007–2008 Season

Date: 6 November, 2007

Score: Liverpool 8–0 Besiktas

Competition: Champions League

Liverpool record the biggest win in their Champions League history against Turkish side, Besiktas, at Anfield. The score was a crushing 8–0 with Yossi Benayoun scoring a hat-trick. Peter Crouch was also a hero on the night!

2008–2009 Season

Date: 5 October, 2008

Score: Manchester City 2–3 Liverpool

Competition: Premier League

A solid season for Liverpool saw the Reds finish as runners-up in the Premier League and reach the quarter-finals in the Champions League. It was in the League that this season's memorable match took place, as Liverpool came back from 2–0 down to win the game with an injury-time winner from Dirk Kuyt! A stunning comeback!

2009–2010 Season

Date: 25 October, 2009

Score: Liverpool 2–0 Manchester United

Competition: Premier League

Goals from strikers Fernando Torres and David N'Gog saw the Reds beat Man United at Anfield in October. The match was by far Liverpool's best win that season. Pepe Reina was so pleased at the victory, he ran the length of the pitch to join in the celebrations following N'Gog's injury-time goal!

A team huddle in front of the Kop

Kuyt opens the scoring at Anfield!

2010–2011 Season

Date: 6 March, 2011

Score: Liverpool 3–1 Manchester United

Competition: Premier League

The highlight of a troubled season for the Reds, this win under King Kenny Dalglish showed what the squad could do when playing at their best! A hat-trick from Dirk Kuyt and a brilliant performance from Suarez gave the fans a day to remember. The Kop went wild and sung 'Happy Birthday' to Kenny!

2011–2012 Season

Date: 26 February, 2012

Score: Cardiff City 2–2 Liverpool (2–3 penalties)

Competition: League Cup

Liverpool are back in the honours as they win their first cup for six years. The Reds beat Cardiff City after another penalty shoot-out, this time at the new Wembley. Stewart Downing was Man of the Match.

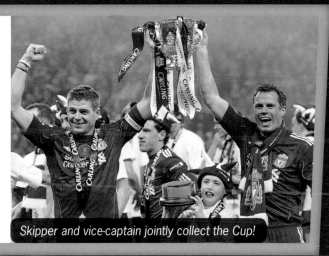

Skipper and vice-captain jointly collect the Cup!

2012–2013 Season

Date: 19 January, 2013

Score: Liverpool 5–0 Norwich

Competition: Premier League

The Reds thrashed Norwich in the League with an outstanding team performance. The newly formed duo of Sturridge and Suarez looked deadly as both strikers were among the scorers. It was the second time that Liverpool had thumped five past Norwich after beating the Canaries away from home earlier in the season!

PUZZLE ANSWERS

Answers

p21 Team player: **False.**

p25 Passport puzzler: **Italy.**

p27 Seventh heaven: **Jamie Carragher.**

p28 Fact or fib? True.

p32 Middle riddle: **Brian.**

p33 Name game: **Showtinho.**

p34 April fool?: True.

p35 Name that club: **Pompey.**

p37 Which one? **London.**

p39 Name the nation: **Northern Irish.**

Pages 14–17 *Puzzles: Kick-off!*

Spot the Ball

Quick Quiz

1. False, Liverpool play their home matches at Anfield.

2. False, he wears the number 15 shirt.

3. False, it's Raheem Sterling.

4. False, Suarez plays for Uruguay.

5. False, Andy Carroll is LFC's record signing.

6. True!

Soccer Squares

3	2	4	1
4	1	3	2
2	3	1	4
1	4	2	3

4	3	2	1
1	2	3	4
3	4	1	2
2	1	4	3

3	2	4	1
1	4	2	3
4	3	1	2
2	1	3	4

Jonjo Shelvey and Dan Agger are in the picture.

Mighty Mix-up!

The players are Daniel Sturridge and Pepe Reina.

Mirror Match

REINA

STURRIDGE

COUTINHO

SKRTEL

SUAREZ

GERRARD

On the Volley!

Picture E is the odd one out.

Player Puzzler

The player is Lucas Leiva.

Flag Tag!

1. Steven GERRARD – England
2. Philippe COUTINHO – Brazil
3. Luis SUAREZ – Uruguay
4. Jose ENRIQUE – Spain
5. Martin Skrtel – Slovakia

Pages 84–87 Puzzles: Final Whistle!

Missing Mighty!

Mighty's Memory Test

1, eight.

2, Number 2.

3, white.

4, three.

5, orange.

6, five.

7, Jonjo Shelvey.

8, two.

Time's Up

A, 3:00 or 15:00. B, 3:45 or 15:45. C, 4:45 or 16:45.

Picture Patterns

1, no.5 shirt.

2, Liverpool FC crest.

3, trophy.

4, trophy.

Pages 56–59 Puzzles: Half-time!!

Squad Sums

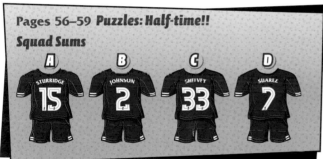

A STURRIDGE 15

B JOHNSON 2

C SHELVEY 33

D SUAREZ 7

Spot the Difference